COUNTRY EXPLORERS

ICELAND

Jennifer A. Miller

Lerner Publications Company • Minneapolis

Lerner Publications Company
A division of Lerner Publishing Group, Inc.
241 First Avenue North
Minneapolis, MN 55401 U.S.A.

Website address: www.lernerbooks.com

Library of Congress Cataloging-in-Publication Data

Miller, Jennifer A.
    Iceland / by Jennifer A. Miller.
      p.   cm. — (Country explorers)
    Includes index.
    ISBN 978-0-7613-5314-0 (lib. bdg : alk. paper)
    1. Iceland—Juvenile literature. I. Title.
  DL305.M55 2011
  949.12—dc22   2009043619

Manufactured in the United States of America
1 – VI – 7/15/10

Table of Contents

Welcome!

Let's visit Iceland! Iceland is Europe's second-largest island. It is located in the North Atlantic Ocean.

Greenland and the Greenland Sea lie to the northwest. To the east sit Norway and Sweden. The United Kingdom and the rest of Europe lie to the southeast.

Iceland

The Atlantic Ocean touches the southern shore of Iceland.

GREENLAND
SEA

GRIMSEY
ISLAND

HRISEY
ISLAND

Akureyri

SKÁLFANDAFLJÓT

MÝVATN

ICELAND

Grundarfjörður

HOFSJÖKULL

LANGJÖKULL

GRÍMVÖTN

THJORSA

VATNAJÖKULL

GEYSIR
STROKKUR

THINGVALLAVATN

Reykjavík

Geysir

THÓRISVATN

Kópavogur

Hafnarfjörður

HEKLA

MÝRDALSJÖKULL

NORTH
ATLANTIC
OCEAN

SURTSEY
ISLAND

HEIMAEY
ISLAND

MILES

0   10   20   30   40

0   10   20   30   40   50   60
KILOMETERS

★ country's capital

🌋 volcano

☐ glacier

🌫 geyser

• city

5

Cool Name, Warm Water

Iceland lies just below the chilly waters of the Arctic Ocean. But warm ocean water flows to Iceland from the south. It heats up the island. Iceland got its name from an explorer who spent a long and icy winter there.

Chunks of ice float in seawater off Iceland's southern coast.

Iceland has strong winds and rain throughout the year. In the winter, people in parts of the country see only two hours of daylight. In the summer, the sun can be seen almost all night.

Map Whiz Quiz

Take a look at the map on page five. A map is a drawing or chart of a place. Trace the outline of Iceland on a sheet of paper. Can you find the North Atlantic Ocean on the map? Mark this side of your paper with an *S* for south. Find the Greenland Sea. Mark this side with an *N* for north. Color all the water around Iceland blue.

The moon gives a blue glow to the snow-covered winter land.

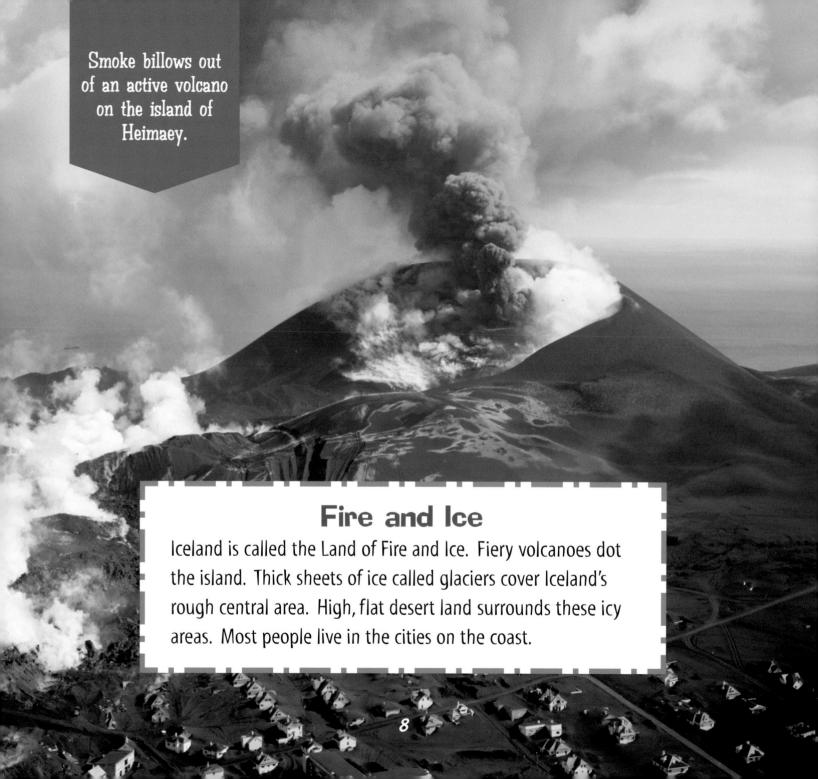

Smoke billows out of an active volcano on the island of Heimaey.

Fire and Ice

Iceland is called the Land of Fire and Ice. Fiery volcanoes dot the island. Thick sheets of ice called glaciers cover Iceland's rough central area. High, flat desert land surrounds these icy areas. Most people live in the cities on the coast.

Some Modern Eruptions

1963	An underwater volcano erupts, or blows up. It forms Surtsey Island.
1973	A volcano on the island of Heimaey erupts. It destroys one-third of the island and creates a new mountain.
1996	A volcano erupts under the Vatnajökull glacier. Melted ice floods southeastern Iceland.
2000	Mount Hekla erupts.
2004	Grímsvötn erupts under the Vatnajökull glacier. Smoke and ash float to Norway and Sweden.

Iceland is surrounded by oceans. Its land has lakes, rivers, and waterfalls. Iceland has more hot springs than any other country. Hot springs are small pools of water that are heated by the heated rock beneath them.

A rainbow brightens the misty air near this waterfall.

9

A puffin flaps its wings on a high mound overlooking the Atlantic Ocean.

Animals

Puffins and other birds live near narrow lengths of seawater called fjords. The arctic fox makes its home on land. On the coast, seals bathe in the sun. Whales swim in the nearby ocean.

Sometimes polar bears travel from Greenland on chunks of ice. But they have trouble living in Iceland's warm climate.

Icelandic Horses

Icelandic horses are short and sturdy. They are perfect for riding around the island. Farmers also use them to help round up sheep.

An Icelandic horse runs across a dry field.

11

Colorful houses line the streets of the capital city of Reykjavík.

A Busy, Clean City

Reykjavík is the capital of Iceland. It is also the country's largest city and has more than 180,000 people. The city is alive with people going to art galleries, plays, and operas.

Reykjavík is called the smokeless city. Homes and businesses are heated using underground water from hot springs, not by burning wood or coal.

Dear Aunt Elizabeth,
Halló!
Today we swam in Iceland's Blue Lagoon. The hot rock underneath the lagoon warms the water. Some people told us the water is good for your skin. I think it feels like a really warm bath. Later, we drove to Reykjavík for dinner. I tried lamb for the first time. It was good, but I didn't like the pickled cabbage.
See you soon,

Hannah

Your

You

Anyu

Blue Lagoon

This statue from northern Iceland honors Iceland's first settlers.

Early Peoples

More than one thousand years ago, people from Norway, Ireland, and Scotland came to Iceland to make a new home. They set up a town that became Reykjavík. Later, they formed a government. A new country—Iceland—was born.

Some Icelanders have blond hair and blue eyes. So did their Norwegian ancestors. Not many people move to Iceland anymore. Most of the people in Iceland were born there.

These children look like many Icelanders, with their blond hair and blue eyes.

Religion

Settlers from Norway brought with them their religion, Ásatrú. This religion has many gods. The people changed to Christianity about one thousand years ago. This religion has one god.

Icelanders attend a service at a Christian church in Reykjavík.

The Gods of Ásatrú

The Norse religion Ásatrú has many different gods and goddesses. Here are a few:

Tór (THOR)   the god of thunder

Óðinn (OH-thin)   the chief god

Týr (TEER)   the god of war and justice

Freyr (FRAY-er)   the god of peace

Freyja (FRAY-ah)   the goddess of love, magic, and war

Iðunn (EE-thun)   the goddess of renewal

Most modern-day Icelanders are Christians. But some Icelanders are going back to the old Norse religion.

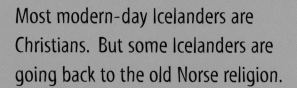

This carved statue represents the Norse god Tór.

17

A carved and painted wooden troll sits on top of a mossy rock.

Folk Beliefs

Some Icelanders believe in trolls and elves. Trolls are creatures from old Norse tales. They are troublemakers. Rock piles throughout the country are said to be trolls caught in the sun.

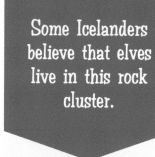

Some Icelanders believe that elves live in this rock cluster.

Elves are friendly and beautiful. They can be seen only when they want to be seen. The main street in the town of Grundarfjörður has a large rock between two houses. It has its own house number. Some people believe that elves live there.

BRAUÐ OG KÖKUR

Language

The Icelandic language is much the same as it was when the country was founded. The Icelandic alphabet is a lot like the English alphabet, but it doesn't use the letters *c, q, w,* or *z.* It also has ten more letters.

Some of Icelandic's unusual letters show up on this sign.

Family Words

Here are the Icelandic words for family members

father	faðir (FAH-thir)
mother	móðir (MOH-thir)
grandfather	afi (AH-fih)
grandmother	amma (AHM-mah)
brother	bróðir (BROH-thir)
sister	systir (SIS-tir)
relatives	frændfólk (FRYND-fohk)

Almost all Icelanders know how to read and write in Icelandic. At school, children also learn English and then Danish. If they go to college, they continue to study all three languages.

A sign in Icelandic and English warns visitors about hot groundwater at a geyser.

Sagas

Sagas are stories that were written from eight hundred to nine hundred years ago. They tell the adventures of brave heroes in Norway and Iceland.

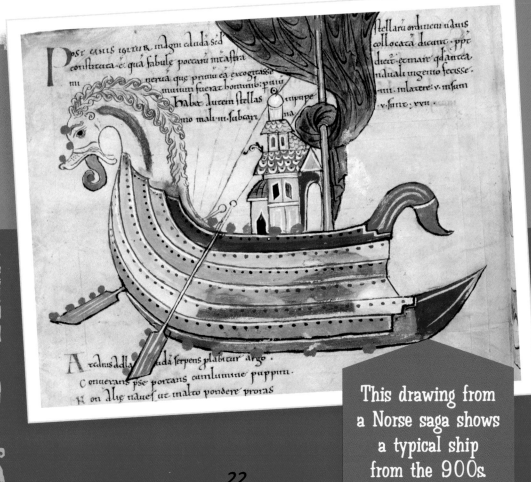

This drawing from a Norse saga shows a typical ship from the 900s.

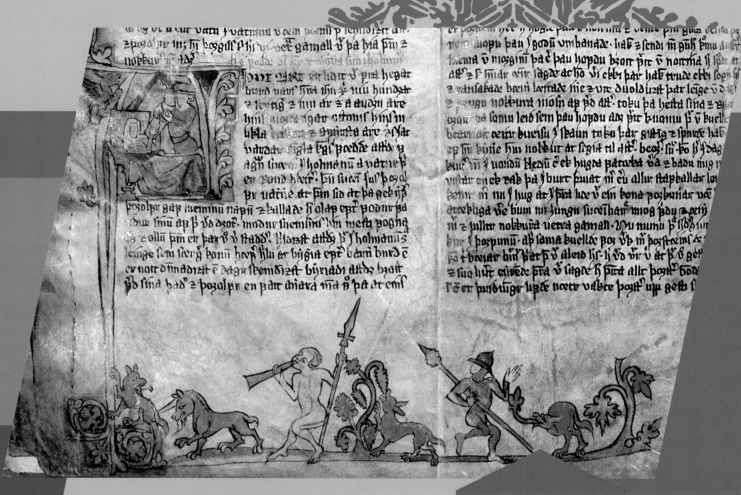

These stories were written in Old Norse. But most Icelanders can read them because modern Icelandic is not very different from Old Norse.

More pictures decorate the bottom of this saga.

The Arts

Books have a long and important history in Iceland, beginning with sagas. Painting, sculpture, orchestras, opera, and ballet are also popular.

These sculptures are on display at the Ásmundarsafn. This sculpture museum in Reykjavík is the former home of famous Icelandic sculptor Asmundur Sveinsson.

Björk performs at a music festival in 2007.

Halldór Kiljan Laxness

Halldór Laxness *(below, with his wife)* wrote more than sixty novels and plays. When he was seventeen, he finished his first book. His books describe what Icelandic life is like. One of his most famous books is *The Fish Can Sing.* He won the international Nobel Prize in Literature in 1955.

Björk Guðmundsdóttir is a famous singer from Reykjavík. She started her career in a band called the Sugarcubes. Later, she left the band. She became popular around the world. Most fans just know her as Björk.

Names

All Icelanders have first and last names. Not everyone has a middle name, though. Most people are called by their first name, except leaders such as the president.

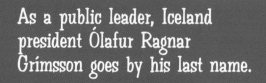

As a public leader, Iceland president Ólafur Ragnar Grímsson goes by his last name.

Icelanders' last names are based on their father's name and whether they are a girl or boy. Adam's daughter's last name would be Adamsdóttir. Adam's son's last name would be Adamsson.

This father's first name will determine the last name of both his son and his daughter.

No Place Like Home

The home is very important to Icelanders. During winter's long, dark days, Icelanders play games and relax with their friends at home.

Families enjoy ice skating on a sunny winter day.

The family is also very important to Icelanders. Many families spend vacations and holidays with grandparents, aunts, uncles, and cousins.

Three generations of Icelanders take a break together.

Mealtime

Homemade dinners include boiled fish, potatoes, and either cabbage, green beans, or peas. Icelanders don't use many spices. Lamb is a common dish on farms.

Lamb and potatoes are served at a restaurant in Reykjavík.

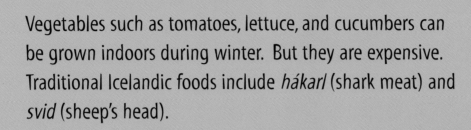

Vegetables such as tomatoes, lettuce, and cucumbers can be grown indoors during winter. But they are expensive. Traditional Icelandic foods include *hákarl* (shark meat) and *svid* (sheep's head).

Shark meat dries from the rafters of a barn in western Iceland.

Fishing

Iceland's waters are rich with fish. Cod, haddock, herring, salmon, and trout swim about. Many countries buy fish from Iceland for their people to eat.

A fisher brings in his catch of cod.

In 2006, Iceland began to hunt whales. Whaling helps the nation make money. But other countries are upset about it. They believe whale hunting is cruel.

Two women in London, England, protest Iceland's whaling practices.

Kids jump rope outside during recess.

School Days

All children from age six through sixteen go to school. At ages five and six, some children go to preschool, but they don't have to. All schooling is free.

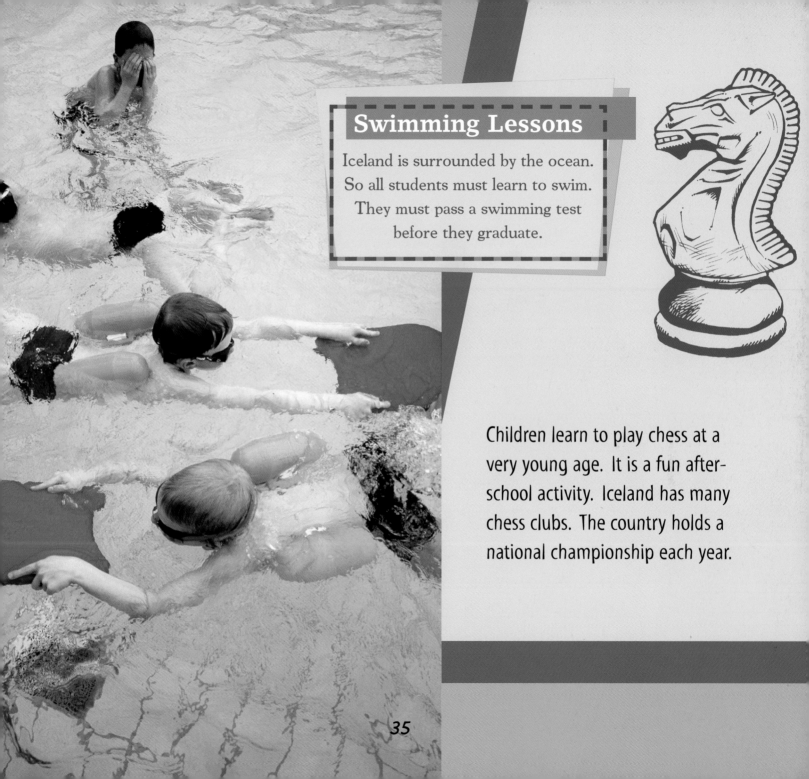

Swimming Lessons

Iceland is surrounded by the ocean. So all students must learn to swim. They must pass a swimming test before they graduate.

Children learn to play chess at a very young age. It is a fun after-school activity. Iceland has many chess clubs. The country holds a national championship each year.

A family watches a fireworks display on New Year's Eve.

Time to Celebrate

Several holidays and festivals add cheer to Iceland's dark winters. Icelanders celebrate New Year's Eve, the Christmas season, Sun Coffee, Thorrablót (a midwinter feast day), and the Easter season with family and friends.

Sun Coffee

Towns that are surrounded by mountains don't see the sun during some of the winter months. On the first day that people see the sun, it's time to celebrate. They gather together to celebrate Sun Coffee. Friends and family enjoy eating special cakes. Adults drink coffee.

During the sunny summer days, Icelanders celebrate festivals like First Day of Summer, Seaman's Day, and Independence Day.

Crowds of people in Reykjavík celebrate Independence Day on June 17. On that day in 1944, Iceland gained its independence from Denmark.

Sports

Soccer is very popular in Iceland. Children learn the sport in elementary school. Professional soccer teams from around the world play in Reykjavík's stadium. Students also learn horseback riding, bridge, and chess.

38

Iceland defenders (*in blue*) try to get the ball away from an opposing player.

The country's national sport is *glíma*, an old form of wrestling. Team handball is also popular. This game is played on a court inside, so students can play it during winter months.

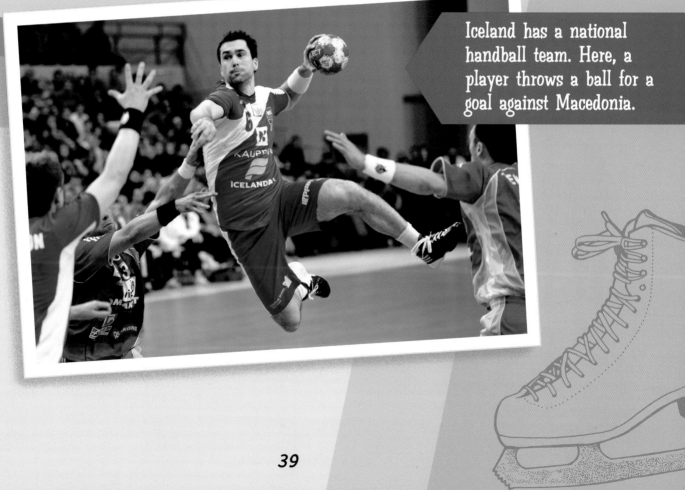

Iceland has a national handball team. Here, a player throws a ball for a goal against Macedonia.

Outdoor Fun

Icelanders love to ski and ice skate in the winter. On summer weekends, people from the coast travel to the center of Iceland for outdoor fun. They enjoy hiking, biking, swimming, and horseback riding.

Skaters have some fun on a crisp winter day.

Geysers

Geysers are holes in the ground that blast hot water into the air. The great geyser at Geysir, Iceland, was a popular place to visit until 1916. It stopped erupting that year. However, Strokkur is not far away. This geyser spouts hot water every ten minutes.

Visitors to Geysir, Iceland, watch the hot water blast out of the ground.

Clothes

Most Icelanders wear modern European clothing. But traditional dress looks like the clothing Icelanders wore in the 1800s. During this time, women wore black skirts and jackets, white shirts, gold belts, and white caps. Men wore knit caps, dark knee breeches, and long socks. Men's jackets had two rows of buttons.

Two actors at a historical museum in Iceland dress in traditional clothing.

Iceland is known for its knit wool sweaters. Icelandic sweaters have a fancy design in white or earth colors.

These girls are wearing traditional Icelandic sweaters.

THE FLAG OF ICELAND

Iceland's flag has a red and white cross on a blue background. The red in the flag stands for the fire of the volcanoes. White represents the country's glaciers. Blue stands for the sea. This flag was adopted as the official flag in 1915.

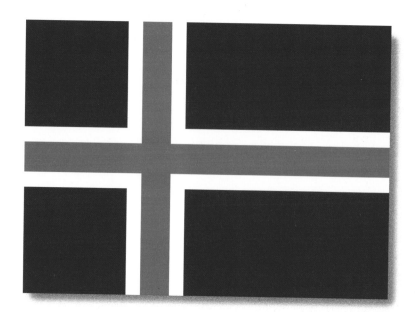

FAST FACTS

FULL COUNTRY NAME: Republic of Iceland

AREA: 39,768 square miles (103,000 square kilometers), or about the size of the state of Kentucky

MAIN LANDFORMS: the volcanoes Helgafel, Hekla, Grímsvötn, and Surtsey; the glaciers Vatnajökull, Hofsjökull, Langjökull, and Mýrdalsjökull; the fjords Ísafjarðardjýe and Eyjafjörður; the lakes Thingvallavatn, Thórisvatn, and Mývatn; the islands Heimaey, Hrisey, Grimsey, and Surtsey; the waterfalls Gullfoss, Godafoss, Dettifoss

MAJOR RIVERS: Skálfandafljót, Thjorsa

ANIMALS AND THEIR HABITAT: guillemots and puffins (coast), whales (ocean), cod, haddock, herring, salmon, seals, trout (waterways), arctic fox (mountains), ducks (lakes)

CAPITAL CITY: Reykjavík

OFFICIAL LANGUAGE: Icelandic

POPULATION: about 304,500

GLOSSARY

capital: a city where the government is located

continent: any one of seven large areas of land. The continents are Africa, Antarctica, Asia, Australia, Europe, North America, and South America.

desert: a dry, sandy region

erupt: blow up

fjord: a long, narrow part of the sea bordered by steep cliffs

geyser: a hole in the ground through which hot water and steam shoot up

glacier: a huge sheet of ice

hot spring: a small body of water in nature that is heated by hot underground rock

map: a drawing or chart of all or part of Earth or the sky

mountain: a part of Earth's surface that rises high into the sky

religion: a system of beliefs and worship

traditional: something that people in a particular culture pass on to one another

volcano: an opening in Earth's surface through which hot, melted rock shoots up. Volcano can also refer to the hill or mountain of ash and rock that builds up around the opening.

TO LEARN MORE

BOOKS

Brimner, Lary Dane. *Geysers*. New York: Children's Press, 2000. Find out more facts about these natural wonders.

Limke, Jeff. *Thor and Loki: In the Land of Giants: A Norse Myth*. Minneapolis: Graphic Universe, 2007. This graphic novel presents the adventures of Thor, Norse god of thunder, and his brother Loki.

McMillan, Bruce. *Going Fishing*. Boston: Houghton Mifflin, 2005. This book tells a story in photos about a young Icelander who loves to fish.

Walker, Sally M. *Volcanoes*. Minneapolis: Lerner Publications, 2008. Learn more about what causes volcanoes to erupt and discover some famous historical volcanoes.

WEBSITES

Time for Kids—Around the World: Iceland
http://www.timeforkids.com/TFK/kids/hh/goplaces/main/0,28375,1018498,00.html
This site has fun facts, a list of Icelandic sayings, and a kids' sightseeing guide.

Windows to the Universe: Norse Myths
http://www.windows.ucar.edu/tour/link=/mythology/norse_culture.html
Visit this site for more information about the Norse gods and legends.

INDEX